To

From

The Good Word

Inspiration for Joy and Fulfillment
In Our Daily Lives

Written by Ralph Rhea

Illustrated With Photographs

Hallmark Editions

The Good Word

Joy

  If we have lost the ability to feel a sense of joy in living, we should try to regain it, for such a sense is vital. Real joy is not false happiness but, rather, a zest for life that springs from an inner sense of peace, even in the face of conflict. It is creative living wherever we are and whatever we are doing and is something the world can neither give nor take away. It is a healthy attitude toward life that says, "There is no need for me to be anxious, for I have the ability to meet and overcome any challenge of life."

Discipline

Such words as *discipline* or *willpower* are not exactly popular because they seem to imply a rocky, difficult road to travel. They are not, however, out of date or irrelevant. The truly organized individuals are the ones who know what their life values are and then discipline themselves to live by those values. Discipline and willpower keep us from drifting with the tide. When the tides of life run as swift and as strong as they seem to do today, we can scarcely afford to drift with them. It is up to us to set our own course of action.

Optimism

Though it may seem naive to some, there are persons who are optimistic simply because they choose to be that way. The cynic may ask, "Why should I be optimistic? What is there to be optimistic about?" A good answer is that we must choose to be optimistic because any other path leads to quiet desperation. It is possible to be aware of the seriousness of personal or world problems but at the same time express optimism about the ultimate outcome. Good, solid answers come with the marriage of awareness and optimism.

Music

➤ When we think of music, our minds instantly turn to thoughts of orchestras, musical instruments, or perhaps the sounds of a birdsong. There is other music of which we are not very often aware. Scientists tell us that the invisible atoms in which we are immersed can best be described as harmony or music. Taking time to still our minds and listen for the music around and within us may quickly put us back in tune with the harmony of life.

An antique collector happened into a farmer's home where there was a beautiful piano that was very old. "Do you play the piano?" he asked. "No," was the reply, "but I have a feeling that there is a lot of beautiful music in this instrument if someone knew how to bring it out." When we speak of individual potential, we are referring to the fact that we all have qualities and talents that we have never expressed. Finding this potential — and expressing it — opens wonderful new vistas of life.

Inspiration

Most people think of inspiration as heightened awareness that fires the mind and emotions to some outstanding achievement, usually of an artistic nature. Since many believe they have no talent for artistic achievement, inspiration is thought to be out of their reach and is therefore not sought after. The result is boredom or lack of vital interest in life. We should understand that we all sometimes receive nudges of inspiration which, if followed, would lead us to achievement.

Courtesy

How we express courtesy or discourtesy may not seem like such an important matter, but quite often it can reveal our true feelings. Discourtesy does not always indicate that we have no sense of caring for the comfort and welfare of those around us, but it can mean that we have become self-involved to the extent that we forget to perform little acts of kindness and consideration that may mean a great deal to others. Thoughtfulness, consideration and courtesy go a long way toward building good relations.

Acceptance

How wonderful it would be if we could accept ourselves and others as we accept nature. We don't expect a palm tree to be like an elm, or a sunflower to look like a rose. To be fully accepted by everyone is undoubtedly an unattainable goal. But it is a wonderful feeling when there is someone with whom we can be honest and can discuss our innermost feelings, knowing that we are still accepted. To find this kind of acceptance, we must also be willing to give it in return. We can only be ourselves if we are willing to let others be themselves.

Qualities

Most of us would like to feel that the effort put into building positive qualities of personality and character will have a greater effect than just forming a good life for ourselves. It is often helpful to think of borrowing such qualities as strength, compassion and love from the universe and then sharing them with others. Few people seriously think that they walk through life alone. It is not possible to express the best qualities without touching the lives of many others.

Often our whole viewpoint on life can be lifted up and improved by simply restoring some of the attitudes we may have once had and have let slip away. We may have forgotten how it really feels to love and to be loved, to see the positive aspects of our life situation, to know the wonder and curiosity of the searching mind, or to believe that the very best of things can happen to us. To restore a sense of adventure in life is to make sure we do not view a beautiful sunrise with our eyes closed.

psychologists maintain

...al binds come because our

... has been too low, not

... standards have been too

... is true, we should then make

... to try to accomplish more.

... particularly true in our

relationship with other people. This is,

of course, not the answer to all problems.

But it is easy to prove that when we

make a greater effort to work with

others and express care and concern for

their feelings, it gives us a sense of

success and well-being.

Thinking

~~ Often some challenge or problem can be met and solved only by using the highest caliber of thinking that we can marshal. This involves looking at the appearances and coming to conclusions based on known premises. However, there is the higher dimension that we often overlook. We need to let the mind work free from bias of precedent or methods used in the past. We should learn to let our minds connect with the free-flowing intelligence available to us. This is a sound, practical way to find new, creative solutions.

Happiness

It is always surprising to hear some person reacting negatively to the word *happiness*. "What is happiness? Who knows what it means? Is anyone really happy?" It is possible to question the meaning of a word until all possibility of a positive reaction is lost. True, happiness means different things to different people, but every person has some idea of what it means to him or her. Moving out of unhappy states is quite often accomplished by simply making the decision to be a happier person.

In these times, nothing is more obvious than the need for a new definition of success. Unhappiness in the midst of affluence is the order of the day. People, young and old, are turning their backs on success defined in terms of wealth and power. Yet there is a desire to successfully perform some meaningful task. Emerson said, "While all the world is in pursuit of power, and of wealth as a means of power, culture corrects the theory of success."

Discovery

Discovery comes as a result of preparation, and then of a real desire to search. Every day we are called upon to try to unravel the riddles that confront us. The barrier is that all too often we fail to smoke out the paradoxes in our lives, to find the truth in situations that face us, or we hit the wrong nail or saddle the wrong horse. To dedicate every day to discovery of something that is real and meaningful brings a new wonder and zest to life.

People are too determined these days not to be enthusiastic about anything. Enthusiasm is passé, it seems. But a life without enthusiasm is like a landscape painted entirely in shades of grey — there is form, but no color. Enthusiasm paints life with the azure of effort, the yellow of imagination, the green of renewal, the scarlet of courage. People with enthusiasm enjoy their work, their families and their fun, and they get more done. They stay younger longer. Enthusiasm is the magic lantern that brightens the most ordinary life with the hues of high adventure.

Thorazine®
brand of
chlorpromazine

Warmth

We begin early in life to express a warmth of feeling with which we relate to life and to other people. The trouble is that we sometimes let the fire go out. A few disappointments, a few failures, a few broken promises by others, and the warmth is no longer felt. By gathering more fuel and rebuilding the fire, we can restore the warmth. With it will come a new perception of beauty and reliability in things and people. There is no need to stay out in the cold.

Practice

Through years of following physical, mechanical rules for life and watching science prove one theory after another, we have come to feel that it is impractical to judge anything except by these practical and mechanical rules. Sometimes the most practical thinking process, however, is to take the time to go past the mechanical and let ourselves be open to inspiration. It is practical to work with the knowledge one already has, but it is also important to listen to the voice of inspiration.

Much frustration and discouragement would be dissolved if we could stop expecting life, ourselves, or others to fit some preconceived mold. Life is filled with movement, change, paradox and contradiction. We would all be happier and healthier if we wisely decided to accept things as something less than perfect but live with a strong faith and conviction that they will get better. Such a perception is the foundation of wisdom.

Movement

The opposite of movement is that which is static, still, or perhaps stagnant. Even when something deeply touches our emotions we say, "I was moved by it." Movement and fluidity are a part of living effectively in our world of today. We must develop more skill in moving from the old to the new without a sense of loss. Imagine yourself in a boat moving with the current, not with fear, but with a sense of joy and expectation toward the experience just around the bend.

Expansion

Expanding our views invariably overcomes boredom or the feeling that life is dull. The feeling of beauty and expansion does not always come by just thinking about it, however. We may see in the distance the high mountains of new possibilities, but we are called upon to walk toward them with new vision and new hope. There are untouched abilities in our lives that can be used for greater achievement if we are willing to stretch our minds and our muscles.

Invitation

One person at twenty feels life is passing him by. Another at seventy is right in the thick of it. Why is this so? There is no standard of age or health or prosperity or anything else to bar some and admit others. Life has a standing invitation out to everyone. But an invitation is just that. It lets us know where the party is and that we are welcome. It does not take us by the neck and drag us there. We are invited to life, but we have to accept. We have to go where it's happening.

Grow

This is a word that can be applied to almost anything, but when it refers to the human consciousness, it becomes most meaningful to the individual. What happens to us in life is important. The real question in life is, Do we take advantage of the opportunity to grow? To grow is to develop, to learn, to increase our ability, to improve our methods. No one is truly unhappy who has a real sense of growing. To stop growing is deadly to the mind, the emotions and even to our world.

Delay

We sometimes wish our lives weren't so full of delays. If we are in a hurry, it seems to take forever for the traffic to move, for the doctor to get to us, for our baskets to reach the check-out counter. On the other hand, every delay can be an oasis of free time in our busy schedule. Long delays provide a chance at a good book. Briefer ones give us an opportunity for some people-watching, or a friendly chat, or just a moment's quiet thought. When we encounter a delay, we shouldn't fume our way through it, but rather find meaning in it.

Reflection

Almost everyone has walked through a house of mirrors in an amusement park. Some mirrors make us look tall; some make us look short. Still others make us look slim or stocky. Our reaction to these images is to laugh, because we know that the reflections we see are distorted. However, when we get distorted reflections from other persons or life situations, we take them seriously. A greater sense of stability comes with the understanding that these reflections, like those in the mirrors, are not the total pictures of what we really are.

Confidence

Albert Einstein, that unusual man who combined humility with self-confidence, was once invited to be guest of honor at a banquet. When called upon to speak, he said, "Ladies and Gentlemen, I'm sorry, but I have nothing to say." After a pause he added, "In case I do have something to say, I'll come back." Six months later he did come back — and made a speech. How wonderful it is to be free from the need to make an impression. This kind of confidence comes from being oneself — doing one's own thing. No one is impressive in borrowed clothes.

Positive

Every thought we think either builds or tears down. The positive thought builds and keeps us from fearing things that never happen. In life there are problems. There are little ones, big ones, strange ones, funny ones, unexpected ones, and even mysterious ones. Does the anticipation of these problems set us trembling, or can we meet them in a positive way? Positive thoughts establish a pattern for positive action, and life is sure to be easier if we refuse to dwell on all that is wrong with our world and, instead, emphasize what is right.

Will

🐳 As we listen to some of the best thinkers and most highly informed individuals in various fields, there is one point they seem to have in common. They may thoroughly outline the gravity of war and world conditions. They may speak of the ecology imbalance that we have created. They may discuss the rapid changes of our culture and environment. But they always add the statement, "We have the knowledge to solve our problems if we have the will." This will is our shining hope, and it begins with each of us.

Goodness

There is much goodness in people if we are willing to look for it. When we observe an act of generosity, an expression of compassion and caring, we should remember it when someone is presenting the thought that human beings are bad and getting worse all the time. Of course, there is much room for improvement and we all need to grow, but we should not give up. To believe in goodness, to look for it in ourselves and others is to see it turning up at the most unexpected times and places.

Excellence

❧ Many people find it difficult to hold a vision of excellence for themselves and their performance in their present life situations. The difficulty may spring from strong feelings of inferiority. Everyone feels inferior at times, but when such feelings are strong and persistent, they cause us to waste our energy on selfish and self-centered thinking. Trying to maintain a vision of excellence for oneself is far more than mental manipulation. By seeing ourselves as excellent, we will become excellent.

Belief

To live without convictions and belief is to make ourselves vulnerable to negation. It is not enough to say, "I believe in that which is backed by overwhelming evidence and nothing more." To look around, to observe conditions and the conduct of mankind may well lead to the conclusion that people are not too good. However, we should choose to believe that we are something better than we have yet evidenced, and that other people are something better than they have yet evidenced. The world itself is something better, and one day the evidence will prove it.

46

Resolutions

It seems that the custom of making good resolutions at the beginning of a new year is not practiced as widely as it once was. Probably it was found that the resolutions were not kept, and the practice was discontinued. It should be remembered that good, positive resolutions, if kept only briefly, are advantageous in making a new beginning. Many people write out positive actions and achievements they intend to try to attain so there is a reminder available if needed. Much has been accomplished by good resolutions kept intact by strong desire and diligence.

Praise

It sometimes seems that praise is becoming a lost art. We hesitate to praise others lest it be thought of as an attempt at flattery. Not only children, but adults as well respond to praise like someone long in the desert being handed a cup of cool water. Praise can properly be called an art because it requires study and practice and a great deal of imagination. When we speak words of praise to others, we not only help them, but we also automatically feel a positive response in ourselves.

Laughter

Laughter is precious. It can rescue us from an embarrassing situation. It can give us a fresh approach to a problem. It can help us keep a sense of proportion. Laughter offers physical benefits, too. It makes us breathe deeper, exercises the diaphragm and makes the wrinkles that are bound to appear in our faces pleasant ones. Laughter even makes friends — laugh and the world laughs with us. As the French say: "The most completely lost of all days is that on which one has not laughed!"

The first time Sister Kenny came in contact with an acute case of polio, she was a hundred miles out in the bush country of Australia. To the amazement of many doctors, the several children she treated recovered fully. When asked what she did, she replied, "I used what I had — water, heat, blankets, and my own hands." Most people are inclined to overlook assets close at hand that would enable them to move toward a high degree of accomplishment. The lesson seems to be, "Don't overlook the ordinary or commonplace. They may contain some of your greatest assets."

Environment

Work in the area of human potential demonstrates ever more clearly that personality, to a much greater degree than previously suspected, functions in response to the environment. Outer environment is important, but we must also become aware of the mental and emotional environment in which we live. Full expression of capacities for love, joy, creativity and spiritual experiencing can help the individual and our society to an environment that is conducive to the fullest development of human capacities.

Openness

None of us wants to live our lives in a private room, closing out the rest of the world. It is the openhearted, open-minded person who sees life as a real adventure. The person who is open to new experiences and sees them as a part of the growing process faces life not with fear, but rather with anticipation. When open to life, we see the potential for good in ourselves and in others, and we love to watch it unfold. Nothing is gained by traveling through life in a covered wagon.

Worth

❧   Isn't it strange how we have to struggle to come to the conclusion that our life has some worth? In fact, the worth and dignity of the individual may be one of the most needed elements in our lives. It seems to be built in us that we desire to make some worthwhile contribution to life, and, too often, we confuse the worthwhile with the unusual and famous. To be aware of the importance of filling a job, raising a child, erecting a building, or adding some joy to others is to find real worth.

Contentment

Our lives may sometimes be lacking in contentment because of the strong desire for material possessions which we have not yet obtained. It takes a lot of living to finally and fully understand that doing is more than getting, that being is more than having. There are some signs in our culture that many are discovering this truth and freeing themselves from the aggressive drive for possessions. A sign of real maturity is finding contentment in the little things of life.

Aspiration

ॐ   There is a difference between aspiration and ambition. Ambition has come to denote a one-track purpose of attaining wealth, status and recognition, regardless of the cost to oneself or others. Aspiration refers to achieving something higher or greater than oneself, free of pretense. Aspiration demands that we search ourselves for the most ennobling goals we can conceive of and then move with compassion and consideration toward their attainment.

Imagination

We possess no faculty that can so quickly turn boredom into delight than the imagination. We may be afraid to let our imaginations go for fear of losing contact with the ordinary affairs of life. We shouldn't worry. There will be plenty of events and people to bring us back to reality. By letting our imaginations take us on flights of fancy, we will lose nothing but gain much. The child who talks with elves and always has a fairy godmother may be closer to the real source of life than we who are so proudly practical.

Love

Music, poetry and the deepest philosophy all tell us that love is the greatest attribute that we can express. We often are hesitant to consider it because it does have so many different meanings. However, there is a golden thread of truth running through all love that points toward kindness, caring and the warmth of being involved with others. Without love, life dwindles and light vanishes, but the mere thought of expressing more love draws forth better feelings about oneself, others and one's entire life.

Progress

To fly across the world in a jet plane, taking only a few hours of our time, may be marked as progress. But we must remind ourselves that we saw nothing of the countries we flew over while the flight was in progress. Many wonderful experiences in life may be missed by going directly toward some cherished goal with unseeing eyes. Real progress can be more accurately described as the journey rather than the arrival. We miss the beautiful experience of walking through a rose garden if we are gazing at the ground and thinking only of how long it will take to arrive at the other side.